The
Power to Control
Mental Suggestion

The
Power to Control
Mental Suggestion

A course of instructions by
Dr.J.G.Leonard.

Compiled and edited by
ENZA SACCO

Published by *I Do Believe* Books.
P.O BOX 25, Moreland 3058.
Victoria. Australia

Published in Australia 2008
I Do Believe Books, P.O. BOX 25, Moreland 3058.
Victoria. Australia.

Rev. ed. 2008

National Library of Australia.
Cataloguing-in-Publication data:

Sacco, Enza, 1961
Leonard, Jacob Goldman, 1861- The power to control: hypnotic
suggestion.

ISBN   978 0 646 49798 3

Mental suggestion. Hypnotism. Persuasion (Psychology).
Influence (Psychology).

153.85

In memory of
Dr Jacob Goldman Leonard.

~ INTRODUCTION ~

This course of instruction about Personal Magnetism and Mental Suggestion has been prepared with great care and deliberation, and needs to be studied with equal care.

Begin with the first page and study each in succession, without skipping a single one. Master the contents of each paragraph and subject in the order presented, so the substance can be repeated intelligently at any time. Do not attempt to memorize; but aim to understand, and make it part of yourself.

To discern the real mind of the author, note closely every punctuation and its meaning, every capitalization and its significance, and by it you will grasp the exact thought of the author, as though he were present, speaking, and giving the emphasis needed at every point.

No matter how simple or unimportant these instructions may appear, make up your mind to follow them in every detail. The greatest things in life are often the simplest.

If you master the Instructions, you will be astounded at the results obtained.

DR. J.G. Leonard

WILL AND THOUGHT

Silent, yet trembling with feeling, the searcher after truth stands at length in the beginning of this century, in the presence of the mightiest of all occult powers of nature, and sadly realizes that knowledge is not necessarily power.

To those whose ambition through knowledge is to reach and control more than human power, the conclusion of years of study and experience is a soothing one, even if forcing recognition of a Divine Element because the possessor of this knowledge may become the effective instrument of this Higher Power.

However, should the aim of the student of Personal Magnetism be to attain the highest effectiveness, it is a curious and noteworthy fact that this Higher Power must only be used for the good of humanity; for the power at once becomes weakened if used for evil or selfish motives.

If, therefore, any such student possesses a natural gift, and uses it—reinforced by this Higher Power, he will indeed become a benefactor of the whole human race.

Yet, if this human dynamo is not sufficiently charged with life-force to enable the 'flywheel' of life to always pass the dead centre of motion or life, it becomes self-evident that some outside power must help this human machine, and must aid in

1

building up its forces, before it can reach its normal condition.

Therefore, if the student carefully studies the following facts, and faithfully follows the instructions given, he will receive this Higher Power and, thus endowed, will be able to perform feats, which would otherwise appear to be little short of miraculous. Such is being daily done by the expert in Personal Magnetism and Mental Suggestion. Hence, the great truth is at last dawning on the minds of men, that man's powers are actually miraculous and measureless! All thinking people now know the power of a man's mind over his body is superior to that of any disease.

There is an assumption in the mind of those who have not given the subject much consideration that Personal Magnetism is none other than Mental Suggestion. There is, of course, a close affinity, but one is entirely distinct from the other; and those who look interestedly into the subject, easily discover the helpful uses to which both contribute.

Scientific men now recognize that Thought is the ruling force in the Universe; and this is bringing the power of the human Thought into great prominence as the possible key to the mystery of the question of ages—what is man?

In the domain of human industry, every wheel that turns is the result of human Will, supplemented by human Thought.

We now know that Mental Suggestion has nullified the effects of many medicines, and that it has stopped the flow of blood at the surgeon's command. When Mental Suggestion, a purely human power, can do this, who can measure the power of the human Mind, where Will and Thought, or Etheric energy, work together in harmony? And if man can control the forces of nature in the human body, to control and remove disease, who can doubt that he can control the forces of nature outside the body?

Personal Magnetism is that strange sense of sympathy (sixth sense), that Soul-Influence, which, when properly cultivated, can be manifested by the possessor and exerted in the fullest degree for his own benefit or that of others. It is an imperceptible, intangible, Magnetic Ether, with wonderful powers of penetration. It is the servant of the Will, and is controlled both by its conscious and subconscious action. The Will directs the course of this wonderful Ether. Its passage from our brain to the brain of another, removes all resistance. We are thus enabled to make an impression on the minds of those around us. We are enabled to place our thoughts in their brain, in the place previously occupied by their own thoughts. We are by this means enabled to dominate the person's actions; we control his Mind, and then his Mind controls his body.

Personal Magnetism can be applied to every vocation, station, situation, and circumstance in life.

It gives a joyous, happy feeling to the mind. It clears up the intellect so that one can readily understand the most abstruse subjects. It gives strength and decision of character, and directness of purpose. It gives love of refreshment, purity, goodness, honor, justice and morality. It adds to the capacity of the Mind and the body in every conceivable direction, and the progress and growth of all these may be constantly maintained.

However, in order to acquire the ability to manage and control both social and financial affairs, or influence any matters that concern us outside of our bodies, it is essential that the one so endeavoring should be in perfect health. For this powerful Ether is generated in the nerve centers of the body, and is carried through the body with lightning rapidity by the wonderful Nervous System, which completely encompasses the whole physical being. This Vital Power closely resembles the principles of life; and it is found in greatest quantity in people who posses the best physical and mental health, and least in people who have physical systems that are almost exhausted. The secret lies in developing and maintaining a perfect physical body. The condition of the body is the reflection of the mind. The body shows, in outward manifestation, the beliefs that control the individual.

The majority of people in the civilized world make the mistake of endeavoring to regain lost health by medication. The only sure cure lies in removing the cause, and helping nature to throw off the disease. Nature alone cures. Drugs only remove the obstructions, so that the life forces may have a chance to do their work.

Dr Abernethy, who began a most brilliant and remarkable career in London two hundred years ago, explained to his patients that *"In case of illness, there are but three things to do: keep the head cool; keep the feet warm; and induce a movement of the bowels."*

These golden rules and every one of them are of the greatest importance. But the three best physicians in the world are: water, exercise and diet. Call in the service of the first freely, of the second regularly, and of the third moderately. Follow this advice, and you can well dispense with the doctors' aid.

Every human being to a greater or less degree possesses Personal Magnetism, and there is no limit to its development.

But the most important questions to be settled by any one beginning the study of Personal Magnetism are, *'Am I well? Is every organ of my body performing its functions in perfect harmony, and under complete control of my Will Power?'*

Very few people fully realize what part perfect physical health plays in their success in life. Without good health we cannot have a strong, active brain.

If the body is weak, the brain will become in proportion, because, as we have said, the Magnetic Ether is developed in the nerve centers of the body;

and if the body is lacking in vitality, it cannot generate as much of the Magnetic Ether as it could if the body were strong. If, then, we are not in good health, we must begin at once to make lifestyle changes and follow a regular system of healthy clean living: eliminating or reducing the burden of toxins to our body, adopting a healthy eating plan (doing away with all 'junk' food), and exercising regularly. If we follow these suggestions, and live up to them religiously, we will, within a few weeks time, be more than surprised at our improvement, both physically and mentally.

MENTAL ENERGY

Mental energy is derived from two sources: food and air; therefore, we must be very careful about our diet! The majority of people eat too much and indulge in the wrong types of food. The human race is suffering from so many diseases and obesity more than any other time in history. You never see any other animal species that is obese and suffering from so much disease unless it is at the hands of a human! Study any animal habitat and you will see that almost all of them have a similar build, and look healthy. What does that tell you? Our species was designed to be lean and healthy like the rest of the animal kingdom.

Ninety-five per cent of all deaths occur from diseases produced through overeating and processed foods, as against five per cent due to starvation. The human system can assimilate only a certain amount of food in a given length of time. Therefore, if we force it to work night and day, by overeating, our health will soon be destroyed; not to mention the extra burden placed on the body when introducing it to chemicals, toxins, and processed foods. If we have eaten a larger meal at night than was necessary, we must deny ourselves the usual breakfast next morning, or at least reduce the intake.

In eating, we should carefully select our food, to eat that which is pure and easily digested. We should avoid stimulants as far as possible, have regular bowel movements, and abstain from all excess.

Half-hour before retiring at night, it is a good idea to drink from two to three glasses of pure water. This may be repeated during the first half hour after arising in the morning. In commencing, this is a little hard to do; but in a short time it becomes pleasing to the stomach.

We will find that our sleep is far more refreshing after drinking the water. And if we are nervous, it will do much toward quieting our nerves.

When we are especially nervous, or exhausted, we should drink a glassful of hot milk, and then lie down and relax every muscle of our body. We mean just what we say; 'we must relax every muscle in our body.' This may seem a very simple thing to do, but in fact it is extremely difficult, because even when lying down, our muscles are unconsciously more or less in a state of tension. If we can allow ourselves to rest in this way for about fifteen minutes, we will be able to get up feeling like a new person. This is the greatest known tonic for exhausted nerves.

Food for the body is transformed by chemical action into Nervous Energy. The blood carries through the system the building material necessary for the body's nutrition, removes the waste and effete matter, and reconstructs the cells of the organism. Good blood builds good structure; and it is air that purifies and oxygenates the blood. Good blood also gives strong nerves, for the blood nourishes the Nerve-Substance. If we would cultivate the Magnetic Ether, we must pay special attention to the nerves.

Strong nerves depends on good blood; good blood depends on good food; and good food consists of that which contains the greatest amount of nourishment in the smallest amount of space, and requires the least expenditure of Nerve Force for its digestion and assimilation.

Weak Nerve Force means weak Magnetism, and makes the person sensitive, weakening his confidence and Will Power. If we are lacking in confidence, we cannot exert the proper amount of Will Power to convey our Thoughts and the Magnetic Ether to the minds of others. The Will regulates the amount of Ether expended and the force by which it is propelled. The Will is the Power that sets all the forces of the brain and body to work, and directs their actions.

But we must distinguish between Will and stubbornness; also between willing a thing and wishing it. Willing a thing is expressing a fixed determination. Wishing it simply denotes a desire; it lacks force, and it is not Magnetic and cannot bring success.

It is an encouragement to the student to know that the Will can be developed and strengthened just the same as any other of the mental or physical faculties. Exercise and use will strengthen and increase the Will Power.; non-use weakens it. To fail to accomplish our purpose is far worse for the Will than non-use, as it completely destroys it and prevents our using our Magnetism. The student must say, "*I will succeed; I cannot fail. Even though I should not succeed the first time, I will try again. I will use some other method, some different means; but I will not give up trying until I succeed.*" Of course, we must not try to do impossible things. The right way to do is to try our Will Power on small things, and gradually increase the tests until we are able to accomplish great things. Confidence and perseverance are all that we need. Confidence comes from success. Every time we succeed our confidence in our ability increases, and we have less doubt about trying harder tests. We must not let ourselves be discouraged by seeming failures, because this would reduce our confidence. And without confidence we would make no effort, but would become like a cork on the waves, constantly tossed about by the Magnetic Influence of every one we meet. We would lose our own Individuality; other people could influence and control us, but we would fear to try to influence them. If we were to reach this stage, we would soon degenerate mentally. Our brain would become so weak that we would have difficulty in thinking intelligently for ourselves. Our real and only protection lies in our having confidence to use our Will Power.

WILL POWER

There are so many serious misconceptions regarding the nature of the Will that we deem it expedient, at this point, to make an explanatory statement, regarding our meaning in the use of the word.

The *Will* is generally considered to be, and is spoken of as, some kind of an independent Entity, to which all other mental faculties are subordinate. Thus, a man's failure to resist temptation is often referred to as his failure to exercise his Will, as though his Will were a separate member like his arm, which might utilize or neglect as he pleased. For purely practical purposes, such a conception as this is often sufficiently accurate. But modern psychology, in its search for a really scientific knowledge of the mind, has had to discard this idea of the Will as purely fictitious. All its efforts to discover such independent sovereign have resulted in failure. It has, however, replaced this old-fashioned myth with a much more substantial and intelligible representative. This Will of modern psychology is neither more nor less than THE WHOLE MIND VIEWED AS ACTIVE, as choosing, selecting, deliberating, etc.

A few moments' deliberation on the part of the student will readily convince him of the accuracy of this statement.

TRINITY OF NERVE FORCES

Before entering into specific and detailed instruction in the use of Personal Magnetism by the student, it is essential that there should be more definite understanding of the great trinity of Nerve Forces proceeding from the nervous system of the body.

The nervous system, as a whole, is composed of three separate and distinct, yet interdependent, nervous systems, whose functions are: the determination and control of all the actions of the body, conscious and unconscious, voluntary or involuntary, together with all the operations of the mind, not only 'from the cradle to the grave,' but from CONCEPTION to the grave.

In the order of their development, they are: THE SYMPATHETIC, THE CEREBRAL, and THE SPINAL NERVOUS SYSTEMS.

The Spinal Nervous System controls all the voluntary actions of the body under the direction of the Cerebral Nervous System.

To the Cerebral is delegated the elaboration of all problems of the mind—of all thought, as originated in and supplied by the Sympathetic Nervous System, as well as to determine and direct all the physical actions of the body through the Spinal

Nervous System, according to the 'plan of action' dictated by the Sympathetic Nervous System.

The SYMPATHETIC is the 'Alpha and Omega' of the human body. It controls all the involuntary actions of the entire organism, such as respiration, pulsation, digestion, assimilation, the growth and repair of tissues, etc. Whether the person is awake or asleep, conscious or unconscious, these processes are unfailingly performed by the great Sympathetic Nervous System.

Its existence begins at the very moment of conception in the uterus, when the individual sperm enters, and impregnates the individual ovum within the fallopian tube during its passage from the ovary to the uterus. Within this minute organism dwells the 'Ego' or the 'Soul' or the individual 'Entity' of the future human being. It at once assumes control of the selection, and the direction of the arrangement of the several atoms to be used in the construction of the individual body, which is destined to belong to that individual 'Ego' throughout its existence, seeing to it that the mental and physical development of that body is in direct accordance with the 'plan' committed to its keeping in its very Genesis. The body will be fitted for the peculiar position in life that it is to be prepared to occupy, and for the particular and special work that it is to be qualified to perform.

All of which is in direct keeping with the statement of the inspired Psalmist when recording the great fact of "THE CREATION OF THE

HUMAN RACE IN ADAM IN THE CENTRE OF THE EARTH,' according to the "PURPOSE AND PLAN OF THE GREAT CREATOR," when He formulated and mapped out in detail the great work of CREATION, of GOVERNMENT, and of REDEMPTION, during the COUNCILS OF ETERNITY, *'before the world was!'* Referring to this special occasion the Psalmist says (speaking in the first person, and thus applying the statement to himself) *"My substance (or undeveloped germinal globule) was not hid from Thee when I was created in secret and beautifully embroidered in the lowest parts of earth. Thine eyes did see my substance; and in THY BOOK all my members were written, which in continuance were fashioned when as yet there were none of them."*

This positive statement has been abundantly verified, both in the history of individuals and of nations. There has never been a crisis in nature, or in the lives of individuals, or of nations, but it was found that there was special provision made in the 'Councils of Eternity' for that special crisis.

We need but instance a few facts in modern history. E.g., there was but one 'Napoleon le Grande,' but one Wellington, one Nelson, one Washington, one Jackson, one Lincoln, one Grant, one Garfield, one McKinley, etc., and each one of these was interested and instrumental in shaping the destiny of this Nation. When the emergency arose, the man was provided, fully equipped mentally and physically for the occasion, fitted from his birth in his training and life, and fitted from his conception in and during gestation, for his special service to the world and to his country.

The only reason for recording and recalling these facts is that thereby we may incite and encourage the student in psychology to persevere in his work, and he will then assuredly succeed.

Personal Magnetism and its consequent and dependent Mental Suggestion are factors in the great study of psychology. Indeed, they are essentials in the acquirement of knowledge of the higher sciences. Let any one, therefore, who is seriously keen of acquiring knowledge of these sciences, or of any science, take it for granted that he was mentally fitted by nature for these special studies, and that therefore he will succeed in them if he perseveres. For if he were not fitted for the special study, he would not have the desire; even as the hungry stomach is a testimony of its fitness and readiness to appropriate and assimilate food.

The chief storehouse of Nervous Energy in the body is in the Solar Plexus, which is in the center of the great Sympathetic Nervous System, and is situated immediately back of the stomach from where every organ in the body receives its due amount of Nerve-Force for the daily performance of its regular duties. It is a physiological fact that we cannot place the point of a needle upon any portion of the human body without touching a nerve filament leading directly to the Solar Plexus. It answers to the SUN in the Solar System; hence its name. The Sympathetic Nervous System is so called because of its intimate and instant communication with every portion of the system, through the Solar Plexus, and thus it is in immediate sympathy with the entire organism, individually and collectively. If any organ becomes depleted through excessive exercise, the 'Ego' in the Solar Plexus is at once notified, and it directs that the requisite Nerve Force shall be supplied from the 'reserve stock' held for emergencies in the 'reserve nerve-reservoirs'. When that stock is itself exhausted, then the 'Ego' has to deprive the organ upon which the system is least dependent for its continued existence, of the force needed for its daily functions; and the organ thus first deprived is the colon or large intestines. This part can cease its usual performance for as much as two weeks, without endangering the life; but the heart or the lungs cannot cease their normal action for a moment, without placing the very citadel of life itself in imminent danger.

Hence, the maintenance of mental and physical health and vigor is directly due to the preservation of the normal condition of the Sympathetic Nervous System, as evidenced by the Solar Plexus. When it is fully supplied with Nerve-Force, through the administration of both liquid and solid nourishment, in due and exact proportion, (neither an excess nor a deficiency), together with abundance of good fresh air and a proper degree of exercise, it is firmly knit up in the center of the body, enabling the one conditioned to stand erect and look every one in the face. But when it is otherwise, the Solar Plexus is loose and flabby, the form limp and inactive, and the voice trembling and incoherent.

The Psalmist David well understood this physiological fact when he said in his Psalm of Depression, *'My heart was melted within me; it hung down like fat in the midst of my bowels.'* He was, of course, not referring to the double-action force-pump, called the heart by anatomists, and which was only discovered by Harvey about four hundred years ago; but he was referring to the 'Ego' resident in the Solar Plexus (in the exact center of the body), which is the true heart of man, even as the heart of the Earth is in its exact center, and the heart of a cabbage is in the center of the cabbage.

A body drained of its Nervous Energy is a body without Magnetism. A person filled with Nervous Energy is a person radiant with animal Magnetism, capable of the fullest manifestation of Personal Magnetism, and of attaining the highest degree of perfection as a hypnotist.

MENTAL SUGGESTION is impossible without an abundant possession and a full knowledge of the use of PERSONAL MAGNETISIM.

THE SUBJECTIVE MIND

Steam or electricty, with all the wonderful results accomplished by their use, would have been worthless if not intelligently guided or controlled. The Magnetic Ether within us is more powerful than either steam or electricity. What we need to know is how to control and apply it to gain the best results.

Before we can apply it to others, we must first learn to control it in ourselves, and so establish the supremacy of the Will over our own Mind and Body.

Now, man has two minds, each endowed with separate and distinct attributable powers, each capable of action under certain conditions; and for convenience we designate one as the Objective Mind and the other as Subjective Mind.

The Subjective Mind is constantly amenable to control by suggestion, but it is incapable of inductive reasoning, while the Objective Mind takes cognizance of the objective world. Its media of observation are the five physical senses; and it is the outgrowth of man's physical necessities. It is his guide in his struggle with his material environment, and its highest function is that of reasoning.

The Subjective Mind takes cognizance of its environments by means independent of the physical senses. It performs by intuition. It is the seat of the emotions and the storehouse of memory. It performs the higher functions when the Objective Mind is in abeyance; and in this state, many of the wonderful feats of the Subjective Mind are performed.

It sees without the natural use of the organs of vision; and in this, as in many other grades or degrees of the hypnotic state, it can be made to apparently leave the body and travel to distant lands, and bring back intelligence oftentimes of the most exact and truthful character. It also has the power to read the minds of others, even to the minutest details. In short, it is the Subjective Mind that possesses what is popularly designated as clairvoyant power, and the ability to apprehend the thoughts of others without the ordinary objective means of communication.

In fact, that which for convenience we have chosen to designate as the Subjective Mind, appears to be a separate and distinct entity; and the real distinctive difference between the two minds seems to consist in the fact that the Objective Mind is merely the function of the physical brain; while the Subjective Mind is the distinct entity, possessing independent functions and powers, having a mental organization of its own, and being capable of sustaining as existence independent of the body. In other words, it is the 'Soul'.

Man, in his normal condition, is not controllable against reason, positive knowledge or the evidence of his senses by the suggestion of another.

The Subjective Mind is unqualifiedly and constantly amenable to control by suggestion. As therefore the two minds are possessed of independent powers and functions, it follows, as a necessary corollary that the Subjective Mind of an individual is amenable to the control of his own Objective Mind, as well as of the Objective Mind of another. Indeed, it may safely be predicted of every man of intelligence and refinement, that he had often felt within himself an intelligence not the result of education, a perception of the truth, independent of the testimony of his bodily senses.

Courage and generosity arise from a consciousness of superior strength. If we learn how to develop our inherent spiritual strength, 'spiritual liberation' will take care of itself.

The Subjective or Subconscious Mind is that part of us, or of our minds, which never sleeps; it is that storehouse which we call 'memory'; it is that part of our mind that stores away all of our experiences; and did we not posses this mind, as soon as an experience was ended it would be forgotten—mans progress would be checked, and he would simply be a barbarian, an animal, such as he was before he discovered for himself, or became conscious of the fact that he had a Mind.

But our minds do possess the power or the ability to remember, or keep all experiences; and it is a memory of adverse experiences or mistakes that enables us to advance in the world or to correct our mistakes, thus proving the truth of the assertion that man's mistakes rectified, lead to perfection. One of the greatest blessings conferred upon man is the knowledge, within himself, that he makes mistakes.

Until he learned this, and learned that he could correct his mistakes, man was no more than any other animal. When we study the memory, when we think of the action of the mind in dreams, when, in certain conditions that come over us, we suddenly recall all the important experiences of a lifetime in a few moments (and this is the experience of almost every one who has passed through some imminent danger), if we would think for a moment, we would readily see that there is more in the mind than the ordinary thinker or writer has ever attributed to it.

There is an unerring way of knowing whether the thoughts entertained by a person are pure and healthy, as every thought we entertain manifests itself in external expressions. Thoughts of disease are manifested by sickness. Thoughts of weakness are manifested by poverty and wretchedness.

All the good that has ever come into a man's life through his own efforts has been the result of a trusted desire, a trusted 'want to.' Nearly every person who is sick has the desire to be rid of his affliction. He has also within him the latent power that would overcome his trouble, if he knew how to trust it. Now, before he can trust it fully, he must believe that that power exists, and if found and trusted, it will reward him for his search, and bring him the blessings he desires.

A man may want and desire ever so much; but until he assumes that the gratification of a want is possible, he will continue to want in vain.

Should he desire riches, desire health, friends or positions, the desire must spring out of that source which gave us life, which gave us comforts; in fact, it does not spring out of any other source; and we know that God, who gave us our life, will withhold no good thing from us.

When we have learned to form in our own mind any secretions that we wish, we shall have secured the real Secret of Success in Life; we shall have learned how to add all things unto ourselves; we shall have become our own master; and, having thus learned how to control ourselves, we shall have acquired the knowledge and the power to wisely control others. For *'He that ruleth himself is greater than he that taketh a city."*

Now, in order to acquire control of the Will, the first form of practice must be mastered alone, and is the art of sitting absolutely still for five minutes at a time, at least to the extent that all movements of the face, eyes, hands and feet shall be checked and prohibited. Wher this has been thoroughly attained, the practice may be combined with further exercises in concentration, of which there will be instructions later on.

The next form of exercise should be practiced for five or ten minutes at a time, and admits of a variety of movements.

While sitting in a chair, turn the hands palms upward, resting them upon a table or even in your lap. Close the fingers and thumbs slowly, one by one, of each hand in rotation, until both hands are tightly shut, looking steadily at each finger as it is closed. When both hands are firmly closed, open them again, slowly, one finger at a time, until they assume the same position as when the exercise was begun. This seems simple; but try it first. Continue this exercise for five minutes, and you will find that you are incapable of fixing your attention with satisfaction upon this very simple procedure. Your attention is inclined to wander, and is neither obedient nor at your service, but chooses to assert itself in defiance of the Will, its Master. You can now understand what we mean by saying that the Will cannot exercise its independent functions until it is first capable of controlling them. *The attention must be made the servant of the Will.*

There are a number of similar exercises bearing upon the muscular action of the Will, and the more the better. In the exercises for the control of breathing, you will find many combinations of muscular movements, which you could introduce in this exercise, and which, if constantly and steadily practiced with the above, will give you the proper training.

24

Inasmuch as the air purifies and oxygenates the blood, the lungs are the gateway to life; and the next form of exercise is the control of breathing, or breathing under the direction of the Will. In nothing more noticeably than in the act of breathing is the involuntary action of the organism shown forth; and, until this training is mastered, you do not breathe as you will breathe, but as you think you are compelled to breathe; such breathing being only spasmodic. Now, you can only obtain control of all the functions by exercising control upon each of the individual functions; therefore, you must breathe as you determine to breathe, centering your attention upon the act.

In this form of exercise there are certain physical actions introduced which are of untold benefit through the development of the body. In the first place, you should assume an erect position, bringing the fingers tightly before you; then fill the lungs slowly by taking a long, slow breath, inhaling for eight or nine seconds; hold the breath for the same length of time, and then exhale it for the same period or longer if possible. Pressing the fingers tightly together tightens up the muscles in almost every part of the body, and is the first position to take when starting out to develop the shoulder muscles. Still keeping the fingers tightly together, work the hands up and down, and this movement will also develop the muscles of the neck as well as the shoulders. It is a great exercise, not only physically, but it gives your Will a chance to overcome your spasmodic breathing, and shows how to properly inhale air into the lungs.

By holding our breath and forcing the air down into our lungs, we tighten almost every muscle in out body, and are then prepared to go through any of the various movements with our hands and body.

To strengthen the abdomen, draw the arms close to the sides and clinch your fists. You are then prepared to draw the chest up and down, keeping the air in the lungs all the time.

To develop the body and chest: clinch your fists as tightly as possible, twisting the shoulders to the right and left while holding your breath. This exercises these muscles, and a few minutes' practice each day will make a wonderful improvement in less than two weeks. As you fill your lungs, raise the arms at the same time: this movement develops the chest. At first it will tire you easily; but a few days' practice will enable you to continue it for many minutes without exertion.

In all these exercises, do not allow yourself to neglect to practice Control of Breathing upon all occasions, and also *throughout all your life*; for this exercise is not for a week, a month, or a year, then to be laid aside, but it is for your whole lifetime, steadily extending the number of seconds occupied in inhaling, holding, and exhaling the breath, according to the more or less swift development of your lung capacity.

The next exercise is a distinct advance, from the control of the physical to the control of the mental functions. In the first exercise of this branch, you should assume an easy sitting or reclining position; then let your eyes rest on some object to the left of you, such as a small figure on the wall-paper, and do this steadily without winking for a minute, but let your attention be entirely centered upon that figure. At the end of one minute choose another object, this time in front of you; and again another to the right of you, practicing the concentration of the attention, unattended with any muscular exertion, upon each object for the space of one minute, and practicing the art of steadfast gaze without winking the eyelids until the attention is voluntarily withdrawn to another object. With a little practice you will be able to concentrate your mind upon anything which interests you; though every human being is developed to that extent to a greater or less degree.

Now fix your attention upon some object held in the hand, such as a bunch of keys, and keep your thoughts upon this object. Whenever your attention wanders, recall it and think of these keys. Turn them over in your hands and examine them. Examine them thoroughly; think about them; think of their manufacturer and their component parts. The world of consciousness exists for you only in that bunch of keys. You are now controlling the wandering propensities of your Intellect, and centering all your attention at the bidding of your

Will, upon the object. Do not allow yourself to become drowsy. You must be wide-awake. Always choose for this exercise the most uninteresting objects. The purpose of these exercises is to develop in you voluntary attention, which, in its highest form, is CONCENTRATION. Therefore, choose simple objects, and practice, until it is easy for you to fix your attention upon any object for ten or fifteen minutes at a stretch.

The next exercise in this degree of development is more difficult, but still more interesting. Assume the same position as in the previous exercise, with your muscles relaxed. Then call up in your memory the face of someone you know well. Close your eyes. Proceed to reconstruct the face of your friend. Put in every feature, separately: the eyes, nose, mouth, forehead, cheek, chin, hair, and the shape of the face. Draw the face on your mind's canvas. Don't hurry. Take your time over this. At first each feature, as soon as you have recalled it, will slip back into obscurity. Your work is to make this face grow, feature by feature; and you must practice until perfect. It is pleasant work, and it is a matter of wonder how strangely proficient in this work you may become by practice. When you are perfect, the face, completed, will appear and disappear at your pleasure or command. Practice this with a new friend for your model every day. It is the development of latent artistic sense, the reproductions at Will, in the form of a picture, of a 'memory impression.' You can vary this by painting landscapes instead of the faces of friends in your memory. Or take in your hand a picture of a landscape, or a portrait, which you have never seen before. Look at it intently for a minute. Then close your eyes, and reconstruct the picture in your mind as before. Practice till perfect, thus developing retentiveness.

Now, center your attention on one of your hands, keeping in your mind the sensation of heat. Impress this feeling upon the point of concentration, the hand; and in a little while the hand will actually feel warm. Later it will show warmth in its color and in its distended veins. This is your first successful phenomenon; and it will greatly encourage you. By your constant thought, you have dirigated the blood to the point of concentration, and performed a seeming miracle. Your mind has influenced the matter of your body by your own volition. Any successful demonstration of 'The power of the mind' is hailed with delight. And while we are masters of our own bodies, we are but children in intelligence. This is readily proven by the fact that so long a system of training is necessary in order to produce this simple illustration of the Power of Volition.

Reverse this experiment, and you will find it still more difficult, inasmuch as the tendency of the mind will be to repeat its triumph and dirigate the blood to the part. This must not be allowed; and you must hold in your mind the sensation of cold and numbness. Soon, under the direction of the

Will, the blood will recede from your extremities, leaving the hands white, bloodless and cramped.

While seated or in a reclining position, with the muscles relaxed, call up the sensation of pain in the temples. Choose a throbbing pain. Concentrate the mind upon this until the temples sensibly throb and ache in response to the blood pressure upon the nerve filaments. Then reverse the experiment, directing the blood to flow from the extremities toward the centers; and the forehead will become cool and the throbbing will cease.

In the next exercise, you must concentrate the attention upon SLEEP. Direct the blood to leave the brain; direct the breathing to become easy and without effort; direct the extremities to become cold; direct drowsiness to appear, with heaviness of the eyelids; direct the thoughts to be of ease, and weariness and forgetfulness. Direct sleep to come upon you. *This is true sleep*, induced by your Will; and when once mastered (and it is by no means difficult, when you have followed this system of training) it is an invaluable ally.

When you have compassed the act of sleeping at will, direct the length of your sleep, whether it is to be of five minutes duration or of five hours. When the Will thus impresses its commands upon Sub-Consciousness, the latter must obey. Direct that you wake up in five minutes; then direct again that you sleep, to wake up in five minutes. Then direct that you sleep again, to wake up in ten minutes... Practice till perfect.

The Mind, acting along a particular line of thought, will continue to act until some other object of thought carries it along another line. And since in sleep only the body is in quiet, while the Mind and Soul are still active, then the Mind, on being given a certain direction when one drops off to sleep, will take up the line along which it is directed, and can be made, in time, to bring over into consciousness the result of its activities.

At night when you retire, instruct your Objective Mind to teach your Subjective Mind during sleep. This will assist in leading you to the right act during the coming day. Instruct your Objective Mind to permeate every detail of your business life with the power or the harmony, which will bring you a righteous success. The quiet of the sleeping body will give its Spiritual Forces even more freedom to act than they would have if biased by intense desires aroused by what your mere reason might deem wise.

Instruct your Objective Mind to give the body that rest which will renew its powers, in order to accomplish results the coming day without strain or effort.

Then, resting in this sense of peace, quietly and calmly send out your earnest desire for the needed light or information; cast out of your mind all fears or forebodings lest it come not, for in quietness and confidence shall be your strength. Take the expectant attitude of mind, firmly believing and expecting that when you awake the desired results will be with you.

Then on awaking, and before any activities or thoughts from the outside world come in to absorb the attention, instruct your Objective Mind to gird you with the right speech, the right thought, the right act; remain for a little while receptive to the intuitions or impressions that come; dismiss all fears or anxiety as to the results, and follow obediently, leaving to the sure revelation of time the solutions of all obstacles and difficulties. When they come, when they manifest themselves clearly, then act upon them without delay.

In the degree in which you do this, in that degree Will the Power of doing it ever more effectively grow.

Don't be afraid to voice your desires. No good thing shall be withheld from him who lives in harmony with the Higher Laws. There are no desires that shall not be satisfied to the one who knows, and wisely uses, the Powers with which he or she is endowed.

In every act during the day, at least every important act, realize that it is the Subjective Mind that is doing the work, and that it has the power to penetrate behind the outer shells of every person or thing with which it deals, and affiliate with the souls of the persons, or that in them which cannot make mistakes. The silent words of that deathless something within, are the words of the Power.

This concludes the forms of exercise of the Third Degree of Development; and you are now called upon to put what you have learned of concentration into more practical use.

You have made the organs of your body feel the Power of your Will; you have governed the function of both the Mind and the Body in some of their manifestations. You must learn to govern them in all. You must exact obedience from them.

While seated in your chair, call up some very distressing circumstance that has harassed you considerably. Go carefully over its details in your mind. Then by the powerful inhibition, command your mind to divest itself of any recollection of the matter. Command your thoughts to become placid; command all unpleasantness to disappear, and command that only tranquility shall possess you. You can do it. Your training has made it possible. You can shut out from your consciousness anything disagreeable at will. Not that you feel things less than before; not that you are any less alive to mental sensation or nerve activity; but that *you are now Master*! You say in your mind what shall happen, and that thing, and no other, happens. Your Will directs. Its authority is paramount. It is Governor.

During the day, go over some habits that have fastened themselves upon you; take them one by one.

Vanity, evil speaking, lasciviousness, drug habits, what ever they may be, and however long you may have been their slave, take them one by one under consideration and put the ban of your Will upon them. The depraved appetite is a creature of the Mind. It is always under the control of the Will to assert itself. Away with them all! Henceforth you must be Master. Let no one pity you for your indulgence, and call your craving a symptom of disease. You are Master of your own fate. Do not lean upon any such broken reeds as sympathy, pity, forgiveness, and excuse. These are not for you as Master of your sensations, appetites and passions. *You are the Master!* Let nothing stand between you and the exercise of your authority.

Break all these habits. You can do it. You must do it before you can exercise the independent functions of the Will. *There must be obedience and harmony within.*

When you have reached this stage of development, you can allay pain in yourself whenever and wherever it appears. No matter what the organic cause may be, and even if there may be good reason for its appearance, you can subdue it and blot it out from your consciousness. Then by your concentrated effort, repair the disorder in the system that found its expression in the cry of pain, and restore harmony to the nerves. All functional disorders and nervous diseases are amenable to the control of the Will. Constipation, dyspepsia, neuralgia, pains of all kinds, insomnia, fears, hatreds, hysteria, melancholy, rheumatism, dysmenorrhoea, self-consciousness, etc., all the commonest and rarest manifestations of disorder and disharmony in the system, are amenable to the action of the Will.

The Powers of Man follow the laws pertaining to all development. They mature slowly by use. They do not present themselves full-grown. They follow the same laws of development in the mental as in the physical sphere. The muscle development by exercise has strength to endure fatigue. The nerve force development by exercise has the strength to endure also, and this accumulation of force grows with development.

If the student will carefully adhere to the directions given him in this course of instructions, the attainment of the highest development of the Psychic Powers is possible.

The provisions made by nature to make every one's life happy and interesting are unlimited and inexhaustible. Life is well worth the living, and is full of pleasure and hope. Our world, if properly understood, is extremely beautiful and interesting; and it is to be regretted that our sojourn here is so very limited.

Nature governs the world by certain laws, which we must obey; and any acts contrary to the laws of Nature are unnatural.

SCIENCE OF CONTROL

THE POSSESSION AND USE OR DEVELOPMENT OF PERSONAL MAGNETISM IN ITS FULLEST EXTENT, IS THE HIGHEST PHASE OF MENTAL SUGGESTION. IT IS THE ART OR SCIENCE OF CONTROLLING PEOPLE WITHOUT THEIR KNOWLEDGE.

The greatest orators have been, and are, men of intense 'Magnetic Force'. They not only knew that they possessed it, but they knew how to use it. They attracted people to them by their Personal Magnetism, and made it their aim to keep the attention of the people whom they were addressing, while they poured out to them the message which they had first studied out, and had delivered to their Subjective-Mind in the privacy of their chamber or Study, during that period of CONCENTRATION with which every person must precede any great performance, whether it be the delivery of a speech, or otherwise. Through their personal Will Power, they used a subtle Nerve-Force, which they exerted to influence and control the minds of their hearers, so as to chain their attention to the Magnetic words they were uttering.

Witness Patrick Henry, Spurgeon, Beecher, Moody, etc. It is told that, when a young man, Patrick Henry spent his leisure in fishing in a small mountain stream near-by his home, where he would sit for hours, rarely bringing any home any fish. On one occasion, some one saw him seemingly watching his cork, from which the fish had long since devoured the bait. He would watch the cork for hours, paying absolutely no attention to anything that was going on around him. Such was his power of Concentration that he seemed forgetful of everything else except the cork. He was concentrating his mind, whether consciously or unconsciously, it makes no difference; and this one of the greatest requisites for successful Magnetic work.

This concentration of thought strengthens the mind and places it in a passive or 'negative' condition, ready to receive thoughts and suggestions from the Subjective-Mind, which is the seat of Intuition, and of superior information.

By all means, then, the student of Personal Magnetism should learn to concentrate his thoughts on one particular subject, and to place himself in a 'negative' condition, in order to fit himself to receive. This prepares him for the time when he will need to be in a 'positive' condition, in order to send forth these thoughts with Power equal to the control of others.

It may be well right here, to explain our meaning of the words 'positive' and 'negative', for they will be frequently used in the remaining portions of these Instructions. It can be best illustrated by referring to the nature of the two kinds of electricity, which are acknowledged by scientists to be operative in every action or movement in the universe. These are 'positive electricity' and 'negative electricity.' The former is characterized by the possession of a maximum of intensity, but a minimum of quantity, while the latter is known as possessing the greatest quantity, with the least degree of intensity. The 'positive', then, we can liken to the lightning flash; the 'negative' to the benignant beams of the Aurora Borealis. The quantity of Magnetism contained in a single ray of the aurora, is so great that were it transferred to the equator and changed into electricity, it would be sufficient to destroy the entire world in a single flash.

When, then, a student decides to appear before a person or many persons, with the intention of influencing them to think and to act as he wishes them to do, he must be *surcharged with Magnetism* (electricity in quantity). And to accomplish this he must, by previous concentration, have filled himself to overflowing with the subject he intends to lay before them. Then his Magnetic Force will stream from his eyes, as positive electricity, to the eyes of the individual or the multitude whom he intends to influence, and his earnestness and sincerity, and desire to speak for their benefit, will be at once impressed upon them all, and will rivet their attention. Then, as he speaks, the same Magnetic Force will thrill their Subjective Minds with the power of the truthfulness of every word he utters, and they at once become converts to his doctrine, and believers of his every statement; whilst the calm, deliberate use of his hands, and the appropriate pointing of his forefinger, as with the authority due to the possession of imperial power, sway his hearers with enthusiasm, as the magnetism flows from his finger-tips, making them all to think as *one man* his *one thought*, which he has thus driven home with sledge-hammer force, and clinched with unanswerable argument! *This is* PERSONAL MAGNETISM at work, and MENTAL SUGGESTION, *the highest and most refined.*

Such and one becomes at once, and undeniably right, a LEADER OF MEN, and the ideas he has thereby planted in the Subjective Minds of his hearers, were they few or many, will take deep root, and bear abundant fruit, to the last day of their existence.

For the attainment of all this, the simple requisite on the part of the speaker is that he shall be:

1. HONEST
2. EARNEST
3. SINCERE
4. ABSOLUTELY TRUTHFUL

Now, in order to exert the greatest amount of attractive influence upon all those with whom we are brought in daily contact, we must be careful to think the same thought of them, which we would have them think concerning us, and we must be in action, what we are in fact. If we would have power over people in general, out thoughts of mankind must be pure and elevating. If we entertain thoughts of kindness, we are certain to reap a rich harvest in kind, because *'Whatsoever a man soweth, that shall he also reap.'* And *'like begets like.'* A smile begets a smile; kind thoughts produce, as a reflex effect, kind thoughts. The philosophy of this is manifest. If we are living daily in the vibrations of love and kindness, all with whom we associate will feel the attraction of our loving and kindly thoughts, and as a consequence, they will be attracted toward us and be helpful to us.

Herein lies the secret of PERSONAL MAGNETISM.

The field is a wide one; there is ample room for us all. We must always lead; we must have self-confidence without egotism, if we would control people.

POSITIVE AND NEGATIVE

In Personal Magnetism, as we have stated, there are two properties, the positive and negative.

By exercise of the positive, as in our battle with the functions of our own mind, we impose the force upon others, so that they do our bidding.

By exercise of the negative, or attracting quality, we draw the respect, regard, and love of others to ourselves.

The positive is valuable in controlling, while the negative is valuable in attracting. Practice is necessary to make our work effective.

We should let no one come into our presence without using our influence in trying to dominate him or her, unconsciously to themselves, or else, as Emerson says *"He who has more Soul than I, rules me."* We must be the one who has the most *soul*. If the person is not passive to our influence, we must use our Power to make him passive; we must send some thought that will dominate his mind, and crowd out all his active or positive thoughts, such as: *"You will do as I say; you will yield."* We must *think* such thoughts as these into his mind for a moment, *"I will control you; I am Master. You will do as I say."* We must speak what we want them to do, in words positive, forceful, and enthusiastic, confident that we will rule, and dominate their actions. We must not yield. We must not doubt. No matter what conditions come up, we must exclude every other thought from our mind, except the one thought that we wish to impress upon our subject. Then we must concentrate our mind on this one thought, and be confident that we will influence him or her; and we surely will. THOUGHT *is creative*. It is a *force*, a *vibration*, a *substance*; and it will accomplish with unerring certainly whatever mission we commit to its care, providing we never change our mind and recall it.

For a second exercise, let us take some one who has shown a marked personal dislike for us and our opinions. We must now exercise both the positive and negative qualities of our Magnetism. We must meet this person face to face and, if possible, have a few words of conversation with him, saying emphatically to ourselves *"I will this person to feel my influence. I will this person to feel my influence, continually. I will that this effect shall not soon be shaken off."* We must also think such thoughts as these into his or her mind for a moment *"You will like me. You will be my friend."* Then your thoughts, so impressed, will find lodgment in the person's mind; and impressions so made upon the consciousness of another are sometimes indelible. We will have thus molded the opinions of this person in obedience to our Will, and the will have also made ourselves an attractive force to this person, so that no resentment will be felt.

For a third exercise, let us suppose that we wish to influence some one at a distance from us; we must say to ourselves *"I will this person to feel my influence.*

I will this person to sit down as soon as possible, and write me a letter."

Frequently this telepathic command is obeyed, and evidence of this interchange of messages will gather in frequency as we continue to develop. But we must be confident that we can do all this. We have but to try it, and we will succeed (or we may take any other thought we prefer, and do with it likewise).

If we wish to find out his character, we must send some thought that will lead him on and draw out his full nature and character. For example, *"I will find out your true nature and character—what you are like; you shall reveal yourself to me."* To make some one return to us with whom we wish to do business, we must use our influence on him when he is in our presence, and when he leaves us. We must think such thoughts as these into him *"You will come back. You will want to come back. You will have confidence in me. You will be favorably impressed to suit the occasion or circumstance."* We must concentrate our mind for a moment, on some thought upon which we wish our subject to act, and then proceed to the business at hand, that is, if we have become Master of the situation. Practice and experience alone will reveal our Power to us; and no one will need to tell us of our success, when once we have felt the thrilling effects of its results. Exercising our Forces constantly, develops our Power, so that we are able to use it involuntarily, unconsciously, and without effort; because the more we exercise our Will Power and Hypnotic Forces, the stronger they become, even the same as with the muscles of the arm when developed by use.

We must hurry through our experiments. Haste only delays the development desired. We must not seek to reach our goal at a bound. Eagerness to skip the necessary preparation is a sign of weakness and lack of self-control. In the slow, calm, deliberate and determined mastery of each step, lies the real secret of success.

In our daily life we should preserve a calm demeanor. In the execution of any act, we must affirm and retain the consciousness that we are using, and have a tremendous force in reserve.

We should avoid nervous, jerky movements and mannerisms. We should aim to make every movement count. Let our motions be in easy, sweeping curves, rather than sharp angles; but we must ever avoid ostentation, of course. The quick jerk of the hand or arm throws off Magnetism, as it would throw off water were the hand wet.

We must not let our mind dwell on the impression that we are making on others. We should always keep our own counsel—follow our experiments persistently and secretly, and believe in ourselves thoroughly. We all have in ourselves all the Power that we need to develop our Personality.

We should observe scrupulously the manners of refined society, and, above all, suppress the element of vanity. We ought never to speak of ourselves unless conversation actually forces us to do so, and then let the subject drop as soon as possible; but encourage others to speak about themselves. In the knowledge of our own latent Power, we have all the flattery for which we can ask. To seek approbation of others is weakness. We will soon learn not to overestimate the value of the approval of others, and we will then receive it lavishly. Such is the experience of all who come into great Knowledge and Power.

Let us ever aim to be a silent FORCE. We should not tell our secrets to others, nor talk of our knowledge. Great men and women are reserved in manner. They speak little. They do not impart confidences. They are self-reliant. They do not lean on others. The weak are ever giving and receiving confidences. They are ever babbling of what they know. *The shallow brook proclaims its presence loudly; but the deep river is silent in its flow.* By reserving more knowledge, we are ever increasing our capacity to receive more, and preserving that which we have. KNOWLEDGE IS POWER.

All the power necessary to bring us all the good that there is in life for us is in ourselves. To succeed, we must be enthusiastic. We must consider that which we have to say to be of importance, or else we cannot have the courage to say it. We must be positive in thought and action, asserting our thoughts with the air of positive conviction, if we wish to carry any influence with our speech.

The positive attitude of mind cannot be too greatly emphasized, when we desire to exert any great influence over others. We always find that 'nothing succeeds like success.' There are two masterful forces in the universe—*Thought* and *Will*. If we use them we will become Masters. We must not allow ourselves to become panic-stricken, or to be disarmed by a little opposition. We must ever stand our ground, fire back with even greater force, and overwhelm all our adversaries by tact and judgment. To determine to do anything, is half the battle. Doubt indulged, becomes doubt realized. To think a thing impossible is to make it so. Courage is victory: timidity is defeat. He who is firm in Will, moulds the world to himself.

THE MIND IS THE MAN, AND THE WILL IS THE MAN'S EXECUTOR. MIND IS THE MASTER, AND THE BODY IS THE SERVANT TO THE MIND.

POWER OF SUGGESTION

The growing interest in psychology and its startling phenomena, will receive its strongest impetus and promotion when the world understands more thoroughly that every day of our lives, consciously or unconsciously, we are leading, molding and controlling character, action, habit and destiny, by the power of 'Suggestion.' Our lives are constant examples of good or evil. And at every turn, whether we would or not, we are directing the current of events into new channels.

PERSONAL MAGNETISM IS MENTAL SUGGESTION.

The deduction from the geometrical axiom or theorem *'Things which equal the same thing, equal each other'* is that. Mental Suggestion is Personal Magnetism. Personal Magnetism is Mental suggestion.

Disrobe either, and you will find the stalwart form of a well-developed, robust, symmetrical 'Will,' a personality whose matchless power, like the true Alchemy, turns whatever it touches into gold—moulds character, changes habit, inspires hope, implants ambition, and commands success.

PERSONAL MAGNETISM

PERSONAL MAGNETISM has three outlets, as we have shown, and we can direct its flow from any one or all, at the command of our Will. These outlets are the voice, eyes, and hands. It is a question, which is the strongest, as they differ in different people. The eyes and voice are most used. When the three are brought to bear simultaneously, the quantity of Ether projected by the Will, at the one time, will produce an influence so strong that it will dominate the mind of almost every living being.

Before the student attempts to use his Power, he should first decide what he wishes to attain. He must bear that one object in his mind, and direct all his energies to the accomplishment of that one aim. He must not let that object slip from his mind, even for one minute. By his Will Power he must direct his thoughts to pass, with the Ether, through his eyes, his voice and his hands.

When using the eyes, he must concentrate his sight either on one eye or between the eyes, at the root of the nose of the person he intends to influence. When using the voice, he must always speak clearly, and with feeling; he must not speak too loudly, or in spasmodic sentences, but should rather lower his voice below the natural tone. The subject will then have to concentrate his mind, in order to listen to him; and thus a great object will have been attained. The student will have taken the first effective step toward mental telepathy. He must not express a lack of confidence in himself by allowing his voice to tremble, for then he would destroy all the effect of his or her previous attainment.

When he wishes to use the Power from his hands also, he must be sure to shake hands with the subject. He must take a firm grip of the whole hand, being very careful not to hurt the hand; then he can give one or two firm shakes, and hold the hand for about a second, then let it go quickly. If he holds it for a longer space of time, the Subject will feel the influence so strongly that he may become alarmed by the sensation, and he will intuitively divine the thoughts of the operator, and his intentions. This is what the operator should, by all means, endeavor to avoid.

If it is desired, the hands can be used to good advantage without touching the subject. The operator should sit or stand within five or six feet of the subject, and allow his right hand to rest so that the fingers will be pointing in the direction of the subject, and then he must *Will* that his desires shall pass through that hand to the Mind of the Subject. This plan, combined with the use of the voice and the eye, can be made very effective. We must always remember that the Magnetic Ether of other people will influence our mind, if we are not on our guard. A positive (or strong) Will rejects the influences that come to it. A negative (or weak) Will accepts the influences and thoughts of others, and thinks they are his own. Our protection is in keeping our Will Power positive. We must make it give out its thoughts and dictates to others. But our thoughts should always be for good, as we have before remarked, because evil thoughts in ourselves are liable to make those around us evil.

After we have learned to apply this Power, we will unconsciously influence those around us; therefore, we should be very careful *what we think*. We must learn to control ourselves, in order that we may control our own Power. The one who can master himself has no difficulty in mastering others. There are no two people just alike in this world, and hence we cannot influence any two by the same method and get the same results. Therefore, we will classify the people whom the student is apt to meet, and wishes to influence, and will direct how to proceed in each case.

APPLICATION OF PERSONAL MAGNETISM

The greatest success in the application of PERSONAL MAGNETISM can only be attained by our first knowing the one who is to be influenced — his characteristics, his strong and weak points, etc. The Magnetism we possess gives us the Power to influence any one to a greater or less degree; but if we do not know the person's real nature and tendencies how can we ever expect to make that person do or think as we wish? To endeavor to apply the same blind set of rules to every Tom, Dick and Harry, who may call upon us for consultation, would be to invite failure in ninety-nine out of one hundred cases we may handle, and we would speedily relinquish the whole business in disgust. The reason so many have failed in their efforts to exert Personal Influence, is that they did not know how to apply it properly.

To gain the results we desire, we must, at all times, avoid antagonizing the weakness or hobbies of our subjects; we should rather cater to his or her idiosyncrasies; if necessary, flatter them. We should at all times strongly have in mind the object we wish to attain, and constantly *Will* that the person shall do what we wish. Whenever the student meets the eye of his Subject, he must bring his Will strongly to bear upon him, especially when shaking hands. By warmly clasping the hand for a moment, looking him straight in the eye, and at the same time *Willing* what he would have him do; also being sure that he will be successful, the student will be enabled to exert a wonderful Influence over his Subject. We can make friends very easily of some people; others are slower in their actions, and it takes longer to make our Influence felt sufficiently to gain their assistance. But we must not get discouraged, if we do not succeed the first time. As the constant dripping of water will wear away the hardest stone, so it is with Magnetic Influence. We are bound to succeed, if we do not permit ourselves to get discouraged.

FIRST EXAMPLE

The hardest subject for a student to influence is one having a very strong, domineering Will Power. It is plain that it would be useless for us to assert our Will or aggressive force against his, for we would inevitably fail. But with such a person we must use tact. We must approach him from the opposite point, until we have gained his friendship and sympathy. Appearing to be humble, we must show our admiration of his excellent qualities, and ignore his weaknesses. We must never give credit to any one but him—not even to ourselves, while in his presence. We may praise or even flatter him, and he will believe us. He is blind to his own faults; we must be the same. He will make many mistakes; but we must not expect him to correct or acknowledge them. We must raise him on a pinnacle far above ourselves, and we will both merit and receive his favor. So long as we show this appreciation of him, he will do almost anything we wish him to do. If we only admire him, and his abilities and his hobbies sufficiently, he will respect us for our good judgment, and will soon obey our wishes. But we must, however, *request* him to do so, saying that we are sure he is the only person who can do it correctly, and this is why we take the liberty of asking him. If we arrange our plans to give him all the credit, we can, by our Personal Power, lead him like a lamb. If, when we look him in the eyes, we express our humility, and our admiration of him, he will be as a toy in our hands.

SECOND EXAMPLE

But the majority of people are deficient in Will-Power. The less they possess, the easier it will be for us to influence them. But we must make our statements positively, clearly, and forcefully, looking him straight in the eye, expressing firmness and confidence, and not letting him think for a moment that we have any doubt of his doing exactly as we wish. But we must never appeal to his judgment, for that would make him stop and think, which would throw him back upon himself, and might defeat our plans. He will respect in us the qualities of Force, Energy and Confidence, in proportion, as he is deficient in the same; for no one admires weakness even in himself. It is natural for such people to depend upon the ideas and dictates of those who have stronger Wills than their own. Hence, we can easily become their Master and dominate their very thoughts, as well as their actions. What we *Will* them to do they will do.

Yet many persons who are really deficient in Will-Power have a certain stubbornness, which is often mistaken for Will Power. We must be very careful while dealing with such, and must use tact and diplomacy—never trying to force our ideas or opinions upon them, for the least show of force on our part would cause them to become obstinate. We must bear in mind that a stubborn person has no strong Will; hence, he is sure to obey our wishes, if we but use tact in presenting them. We must ask him if he does not think so and so. He will usually think as we would have him think. If he should not, we had better say no more at that time, but wait a better opportunity, and present our case in a different way, yet always seeming to depend upon his judgment.

We must never neglect the important part, i.e., keep our eyes on his, and keep our desires constantly in mind.

THIRD EXAMPLE

If the person is at all Intuitive, we can accomplish our purpose by being in the same room with him, without talking to him, providing we concentrate our Mind upon him and *Will* that he obeys our wishes—always thinking of what we wish him to do. Telepathically he will get our wishes, and will believe that they are his own. A wonderful amount of influence is produced in this way. In fact, we have found it a very satisfactory method.

It is better for us to sit behind the person, so that our eyes do not meet his, and then look at the base of the brain while transmitting our wishes. This is really WIRELESS TELEGRAPHY.

It frequently happens that a person in a crowded assembly discovers another person seated ahead of him, and wishes that he would recognize him. After looking at him intently for a few minutes, the second party begins to manifest restlessness in his seat, and finally turns and looks directly at the first party. If, then, so much can be done by merely wishing it, how much more can we do if we concentrate our Mind upon the Subject, and confidently and calmly *Will* him to obey our wishes! He will assuredly do so. Providing that we permit no doubt of our success to creep into our mind.

FOURTH EXAMPLE

It may be that sometime we may need to influence some one whom we recognize as possessing a violent temper.

In dealing with such a person we must talk quietly, and not allow ourselves to get excited, using a modulated, smooth tone of voice. This has a quieting effect on the nerves and temper of the subject. *Temper is the result of uncontrolled emotions;* we must therefore be careful not to play too much upon the feelings of such an easily wrought up party. What we must do is to produce a soothing, quieting effect upon his nerves; otherwise he cannot think intelligently; and until he does we can do nothing with him. If we keep our object prominent in our own mind, he will get to think as we do. His reason and Will Power are not properly balanced. Therefore, if we keep him cool, we will have but little difficulty in getting him to accede to our wishes. Yet if he should lose control of his temper, it is useless to argue with him—that is similar to shaking a red flag at a bull, but we should leave him for the time being. He will think differently the next time we meet him. Our calm and quiet statement will have been more or less unconsciously meditating upon our statement during our absence, and will be prepared to agree with us. We will surely succeed on the next occasion, for we will have learned how to avoid arousing his feelings; and as he is deficient in Will Power, he will eventually yield to us and adopt our view as his own. Whereas, had we argued with him on the former occasion, endeavored to force him to accept our view as correct, he would thereafter, during his entire lifetime, have never seen us again without having the entire antagonism of his nature aroused against us, and manifested in prompt and vigorous opposition to any and every statement we might make.

FIFTH EXAMPLE

The easiest people in this world to influence are the vacillating and procrastinating ones. Their Will is flexible, and we can readily get them to our way of thinking. But we must make use of them at once, or, by tomorrow, some one else may have caused them to change their decisions. We cannot rely upon them when they are out of our presence; *but we can control them absolutely when they are with us.* They are rather cowardly, and fear trouble; hence, to avoid it, they will at times also avoid telling the truth. They are very fine machines; but they need steam, and an engineer to make them useful. It then behooves us to become their engineer. We can direct their thoughts and actions, if we show confidence and appeal to their sympathies. A tale of woe, or a sad story, told in the tremulous tones of real grief, is often very effective with them. Being ruled by their hearts instead of their heads, we at once know how to appeal to them. They are easy subjects, and usually lack the moral stamina to refuse our bidding. They would rather do what we wish, than cause any trouble, or seem ungrateful.

SIXTH EXAMPLE

If the character indications of the person we wish to influence are that he is naturally extravagant in ideas, and in the use of money, we need have no trouble in getting from him anything we want. We have but to appeal to him as in the previous case, with the exception that instead of wasting our time in asking for small favors, *we must ask for all we want*. By keeping our eyes well fixed on his, and assuming a friendly air, we cannot fail; he will give us his last dollar.

SEVENTH EXAMPLE

If we need to influence one whom we can see, by reading his mental characteristics, is inclined to be interested in the mystic, occult and supernatural, we should, in addition to observing the general directions for his case, also become very much interested in the occult, and all kindred subjects. And no matter how improbable his ideas or beliefs may be, we must not dispute his word in any of them, but must agree with him, and show him that we are eager to have him tell us more about such things. We must marvel at his wonderful knowledge and deep research. He will soon become our friend, and will grant all our wishes. It is not necessary that our plans should be very practical; in fact, if they are a little mysterious, he will be the more influenced by them, for he prefers the 'unreal' to the 'real'. He will exaggerate; but only because he believes his ideas are right. Our cause will not be the least harmed by exaggerating and elaborating a little, provided we use good and expressive language, well chosen, to the point, and clear in its meaning, being sure that that every sentence closes with a verb or a noun, *but never, under any circumstances, with a preposition, or any other part of speech.* When dealing with this class of people we must always remember that, a mere plain, cold statement of facts will not have the proper effect upon him. We would better not try at all to influence him.

EIGHTH EXAMPLE

If we have to deal with one who is nervous, critical and skeptical, then we have met one who has an exalted opinion of his own ideas, and can only see flaws in those of other people. This is an extremely difficult case to handle; and it will require that we should use all the diplomacy and tact we possess in order to win. We must devote our entire attention to the quieting of his nerves, which we can do by directing our mind and thoughts to that purpose. We must avoid opposing him or criticizing his statements, even if they are incorrect. If we oppose him he is certain to become irritable, and then we will have a poor opportunity to succeed with him. He is a hard case to handle; but we must not get discouraged. We may not accomplish our purpose until we have tried several different times; but perseverance will win, so we must not give up. The plans we place before him must be well considered; and every possible flaw must be eliminated. But even then, we must be prepared to hear him criticize and tear to pieces every one of our fond hopes. He will suggest changes in many directions. But if we can only agree with him and gradually bring to see that our ideas are his, and give him the credit, we will meet with no further trouble in managing him.

NINTH EXAMPLE

Now, when dealing with a person who is practical, truthful and intelligent, we must be prepared to make practical and logical statements. We must be truthful, and never exaggerate. We must look him straight in the eyes with a frank, honest expression; and we must keep our gaze steadfastly fixed upon him, for any tendency to look to in other directions while talking with him, will make him lose confidence in us; we must never forget that. The secret of our success with him is gaining his confidence. He is certain to deal squarely and honestly with us. Whatever he promises to do, he will do; we can always trust him to fulfill his promises at the very time he has agreed. We must be careful not to flatter him directly; but we can have a great effect upon him by showing, in our actions, our appreciation of his judgment and opinions. We must make our statements and requests clear and to the point, speaking quietly, but firmly, and never making any statements that we are not fully prepared to prove. Our diction must be terse and direct. Talking, only for the sake of multiplying words, is repellent to him; mere verbiage is disgusting. We must say what we have to say, in as few words as possible, and then stop. He will put all the statements together, and adjudge their value.

TENTH EXAMPLE

If we have any original scheme or plan, and need some one to assist us in floating it, we must select a man whose characteristics reveal to us that he is a man of independence (the spatulate type of finger, broad and flat like a painter's brush) a man who loves action and is very energetic. In dealing with him we must be more enthusiastic and emotional than logical, and must quickly state our proposition. He is always on the lookout for something new; and no scheme is too large for him to undertake. He lives on his feelings, and not on his judgment. He makes many errors; but he is a worker while he is at it, and therefore we must do a great deal of talking and get him to talk also. It is not well to let him think too much, or get interested in any other scheme, for he is always interested most in the last scheme presented. So long as we can keep him enthused, even if we must draw upon our imagination to do so, he will work for us night and day. We must not neglect to keep our desire constantly in mind, and must keep with him as much as possible, in order that we may convey our ideas to him 'telepathically' and make him use them as his own.

ELEVENTH EXAMPLE

There are some persons so constituted by birth and training that they are naturally morbid and melancholy; they *like* to be sad; they are *built that way*. The entire world seems against them; nothing appears bright or cheerful; gayety and frivolity make them shudder. With these people we must appear, temporarily at least, at a loss to know what further to do in order to make headway in life. We must think up some of our hard-time experiences, and tell it to them with a depth of sadness in our voice, and sadness in our eyes. The more we can sympathize with them, the more sympathy we will get from them in return; for *'misery likes company.'* When we have reached this point we will have much less difficulty in obtaining from them what we wish.

TWELFTH EXAMPLE

With a person who is very particular about details, is full of system and method, we must also be particular in every direction, in every detail of our dress, our deportment and our speech. He will take us all in at a glance; and if we are neat in our appearance, spotlessly clean, gentlemanly in action, with self-possessed manner, and a step and voice denoting firmness and a full supply of Nerve-Force, we cannot fail to make good impression, and he will pay courteous attention to what we say.

THIRTEENTH EXAMPLE

Then there are those, and many of them, who pay no attention to detail. They are just the opposite of the preceding character. They are careless in their dress, and have a natural dislike for the minutiæ of life. They grasp a subject as a whole, and have no time to waste on the little things. We will not need to pay special attention to our dress before approaching them. In fact, a too close and manifest attention to the detail of our personal 'make-up,' will induce them to esteem us as 'finicky,' and 'foppish,' and as paying more attention to our appearance than to the real and substantial things in life. When we do meet them, we must come to the point at once, make our statements quickly and not use any unnecessary language. We must speak rapidly as possible, by which we mean, not the rapid utterance of our words, but the speedily reaching the end of our statement; because, no matter how quickly we may have presented our plan, *they will have intuitively 'sensed' our statement before we have gotten half through.* These people are remarkable characters. And if we have kept our eyes on theirs, and our plans well in mind while speaking, they will be ready to give us the answer we desire as soon as we have ceased.

FOURTEENTH EXAMPLE

It seems scarcely necessary to say that should our subject have the *Material Instinct* strongly manifest, and be a lover of good living, the quickest way to reach his heart is through his stomach. We must invite this one to the best dinners money can buy, offer him good cigars, and show ourselves to be men of the world in general. He will quickly decide that we are the 'right kind', and will anxious to show that he is more generous even than we are. This is, then, the moment for which we have been working and waiting. It will not be wise for us to tell him what we want, and ask him to aid us, etc., but we should rather, in a sort of confidential way, lay out our plans before him, and incidentally remark (which would be really a 'suggestion') that we would like to find some one who could do such and such for us. It is not likely that he will say anything at the time, but we will have planted the thought, as a seed, and it will take root and germinate. Then sometime, when we least expect it, he will surprise us by granting our wishes. He likes to do things in that manner; in fact, *that is the way in which HE is built*. When he does this, we must be profuse in our expressions of thanks, and demonstrative in the manifestation of our appreciation of his courtesy. He will be quite ready then to grant us any other favor we might wish, for another good dinner and for generous applause.

FIFTEENTH EXAMPLE

The information we can gain while shaking hands with people is a wonderful assistance to us in properly applying our PERSONAL MAGNETISM. If we find the hand soft under pressure, we are aware that he is constitutionally lazy, and also selfish at heart. We can easily influence him; but he must grant our favor at once, or we will not get it. He may seem very kindly toward us, and promise to do what we ask of him, but as soon as we are out of his sight he will forget us, and we will lose our influence over him until he again comes before us, when he will have all manner of excuses to offer as to why he failed to do as he promised. But if he had one hundred excuses, the whole of them put together would not amount to one good and sufficient reason for his failure. We can never depend upon him when he is out of our sight; and a good rule to adopt is to never waste any time upon such a person, unless absolutely unavoidable. The same rule also applies to those who merely place the tips of their fingers in your hand, but make no response whatever to your grasp, and give no sign of movement. These people are heartless and selfish, and care only for their own precious interest. Time spent with them is wasted. We always feel like throwing the hand of such a person away from us the moment we touch it, for there is such a strong feeling of repulsion, which instantly strikes our Solar Plexus and causes a desire to have nothing further whatever to do with them.

SIXTEENTH EXAMPLE

If we would influence persons of the opposite sex through their affections, we must follow the instructions pertaining to their characteristics, and then be careful to be not too demonstrative. Human nature is very strange; it always wants what is kept from it, or what it fears it cannot get. Whatever is obtained easily is esteemed of no value. We may show every possible kindness, courtesy and affection; but we must avoid direct expressions of love, until we are sure we have won the object of our desire.

It is a comparatively easy task to influence one of the opposite sex, because we have both animal and Personal Magnetism at our disposal. If we wisely use these two, we will not fail once in a hundred times, that is, if we are honest and sincere in our desires. Granted these foundation factors, then our success will be measured by the amount of Personal Magnetism we have developed, and by the degree of control we shall have acquired over ourselves when we commence to use this power. And the more we use it the stronger will we become, both physically and mentally.

LUCKY OR UNLUCKY ?

If the student faithfully follows these instructions, there are few positions too great for him to reach and to satisfactorily fill. *These rules have been followed by all successful people*. But they have been *Intuitively* performed by them, and not consciously. They did not know, and could not explain, how or why they climbed the 'ladder of success.' They were simply called 'lucky', and there the matter rested. But it is not luck. It is the intelligent use of Power which is possessed by all to a greater or less degree, but which is not used so as to bring success. The reason is that they have never possessed the Key to the innermost Secrets of Human Nature. That Key is herein supplied. As soon as we have studied, fully comprehended, and faithfully carried out these rules and exercises, so as to have made them a part of ourselves, we have then acquired the Power to discover the strong and weak points in the character of every one we meet, and to instantly know how to attack the weakest point. It is then like going through an open door, instead of having to batter down the walls.

SUMMARY

It is not necessary that we should go into further detail. We have already shown a sufficient diversity of action and treatment to enable every one of average intelligence to adapt themselves at any time to the then particular case on hand.

The main point to keep in view is to remember that 'birds of a feather stick together,' and therefore we must sympathize with the plans of every one, and, above all, show ourselves good listeners. It is amazing how great an effect this little action has upon every one. Whatever may be the hobby of the individual, we must express our desire to know more about it. Our opinions must be in favor of his ideas. Then he will cultivate our society; and, believing that we have good judgment, he will be the more easily influenced by the 'suggestions' we later make. The great secret of all personal influence is to make the other party admire our judgment. And this is most easily done by praising his Judgment. Ninety-nine per cent of the human race possesses sufficient vanity to make them believe us when we compliment them.

IMPORTANT

A single reading of these instructions by the student will not suffice for him to acquire the Power he is seeking to attain, nor will it suffice to even enable him to pass intelligent judgment upon these lessons, as to whether through their study he can really attain the degree of influence over his fellow men that he desires. He must not approach this study in the spirit of CRITICISM, but in the spirit of FAITH. He must eliminate every element of doubt from his mind, and believing that he *can*, resolutely determine that he *will* secure for himself the wondrous power of controlling the actions of men by leading their mind to think upon the line he directs. Hence these lessons must be read, and studied, and pondered, over and over again, until we thoroughly UNDERSTAND them, and are able to repeat their substance in our own language, so that we convey the same ideas to another without having any recourse to these pages. And then we must practice! and practice!

Such careful STUDY, and Psychic UNDERSATNDING, and faithful PRACTICE will unfailingly raise the student to the Pinnacle of SUCCESS IN LIFE. Both socially and financially, without any reliance whatsoever upon a single element of 'chance' or 'luck.' His position of eminence in the world, and of Psychic Power, will then be entirely due to MERIT.

A FEW WORDS IN CLOSING

Let not the student imagine that the foregoing Lessons are an attempt to teach 'HOW TO ATTAIN THE UNATTAINABLE.' Impossible as it may appear that any single human being can ever wield such surpassing influence over his fellow creatures as is herein portrayed, it is nevertheless a fact that: not only can this be done now, but more, far more than we can even conceive, is yet to be accomplished by Man, *as Man*.

These lessons simply teach the science of 'HOW TO BE ALL THINGS TO ALL MEN.' But, having once mastered these Psychic Teachings, the Human Mind will then be in position to attain still greater heights of Psychic Power. Man will not know all that is to be known when these laws of Psychic Phenomena are mastered. He will not even know the 'ABC' of psychology. Just as human vision is circumscribed to those on the earth, but is vastly enlarged in scope as the body is raised above the earth (the greater the height, the more extended the view), so in the problem of Psychic Research and Control, *'The more we learn, the less we know.'* That is, in proportion as we attain mental heights, the greater and grander become our conception and perception of the psychic heights yet to be explored. And when these are explored, they will be found to be but 'stepping-stones' to still greater heights, also, yet to be explored. And so it will continue through time, until that period will arrive when *'we shall know as we are known.'*

In the 'COUNCILS OF ETERNITY,' to which we have heretofore alluded, it was determined that MAN should be made 'a little lower than the angels' (or, a little while inferior to the angels, Heb.), but that he should ultimately 'have all things (placed) under him,' and be 'crowned with glory and honor.' Now the 'all things' here mentioned means ALL THINGS, i.e., all the forces of the universe shall be ultimately under his control. All the Physical and Mental and Spiritual Forces will be at his disposal for good. Even the Angels themselves will then, be inferior to Man. Man will then, through his ultimate Psychic Power, be able to control all the physical forces of nature, so as to transport himself through space, as required, at Will, controlling the LAWS OF GRAVITATION, OF ATTRACTION, and of REPULSION, etc., and hence pass *through the air without wings.*

This is the great THOUGHT and FACT that we have in our mind in writing these 'closing words,' and which we hereby and herein desire to impress and 'write upon' the Psychic Mind of the student of these Lessons. The idea of the great masters of art in always painting Angels with wings, on the presumption that because birds need wings in order to fly, therefore Angels must necessarily need wings in order to travel through space is grossly carnal and contrary to fact.

In patriarchal times, Angels appeared to the prophets of old, and to men, and walked and talked with them '*as Men.*' And if the ULTIMATE AND IDEAL MAN is to be above even the Archangel, then indeed will he also not need wings in order to visit the different worlds in space. Such is to be 'THE ULTIMATE DESTINY AND POWER OF THE HUMAN RACE.'

But such attainment is not to be, and cannot be, in a single day. All development is a 'Process of Growth.' In mental and Psychic Growth, it is on the principle of '*line upon line, and precept upon precept.*' Hence, let us manfully begin at the foot of the ladder, and mount, even if laboriously, still persistently, step by step, until we have attained the heights which can only be gained by the eager and earnest SEARCHER AFTER ALL TRUTH.

~ NOTES ~

~ NOTES ~

~ NOTES ~